Shadows of The Real

K. K. Srivastava, born in 1960 in Gorakhpur, in Uttar Pradesh, studied masters in Economics from Gorakhpur University in 1980. He joined the Indian Audit & Accounts Service in 1983 and is currently working as Principal Accountant General (Audit), Madhya Pradesh. He has two volumes of poetry titled, *Ineluctable Stillness* (2005) and *An Armless Hand Writes* (2008), to his credit.

Praise for K. K. Srivastava's other two books
Ineluctable Stillness **and** *An Armless Hand Writes*:

'Srivastava employs divergent and expansive rhythms and an opening out of sense to myriad possibilities......the visionary quality in these poems can seem astonishing in its range, its depth, its complexity. The rootedness in the local landscape is no limitation; a connectedness to history, literature and humanity, runs through these poems.' —Patricia Prime in *Re-Markings*

'A rare courage suffuses his poems, the courage to challenge commonplace notions.....He is not a genteel poet, he is a disturbing poet, intent on unravelling the human mind of its false preoccupations, of its delusive hypocrisy masked as genuine emotions.' —The *Hindustan Times*

'*An Armless Hand Writes* is comparable to *The Waste Land*... Most certainly this book will pose intellectual riddles for the snobs and hypocrites of present society' —*The Pioneer*

'[His poetry is]...well-aroused, tormenting[...]the length of his reading and the breadth of his encyclopedic memory impress....' —*The Little Magazine*

'At times wry, often intriguing[...]his anthologies are like splintered abecedarian, in which ideas and themes keep flowing in an individualistic and disorderly pattern. In these daringly beautiful poems, there is the feeling of disorientation—but that is in line with what life is really like......constantly being buffeted by the winds of new ideas.' —Anoop Verma in *Alive*

'*An Armless Hand Writes* contains a whole host of life impressions offered with deep wisdom and truth and with the look on essential things-touching and thought provoking. All on a high linguistic level.' —Prof Kurt F. Svatek, Nobel prize nominee for literature from Austria

Shadows of The Real

A Collection of Poems

K. K. Srivastava

RUPA

Copyright © K. K. Srivastava 2012

First Published in 2012 by
Rupa Publications India Pvt. Ltd.
7/16, Ansari Road, Daryaganj,
New Delhi 110 002

Sales Centres:

Allahabad Bengaluru Chennai
Hyderabad Jaipur Kathmandu
Kolkata Mumbai

All rights reserved.
No part of this publication may be reproduced, stored in a
retrieval system, or transmitted, in any form or by any means,
electronic, mechanical, photocopying, recording or otherwise,
without the prior permission of the publishers.

ISBN: 978-81-291-2011-3

10 9 8 7 6 5 4 3 2 1

K. K. Srivastava asserts the moral right to be
identified as the author of this work.

Printed and bound in India by
Repro Knowledgecast Limited, Thane

Contents

Foreword ix
Preface xi

Our Being Us 1
That Night 18
Stray Thoughts 20
Between Night and Morning 23
Fate 24
Time's Emptiness 25
Blindness 34
Chanakya Puri of New Delhi 35
An Insomniac's Dilemma 39
Sins 40
Mental Asylum and Poetry 41
A Doubt 42
A Mirror 43
Nothing Left to Tell 45
A Beggar 47
Contemplation 48
Faces 49
Mind 51

Decisions	53
A Day	55
A Thought	56
Hopes	58
Success	59
Whispers	61
Love is Not Deception	62
Voids	64
Lonely Travellers Go Astray	65
Fog	67
Sealed Remembrance	68
From Within	70
Image of Life	72
Through Time	74
A Sketch Made in December	76
Depression	78
A Woman	79
Afternoon Musings	81
Human Illusions	82
Melancholy	98
Conflicts	99
Mind and Desires	100
Contemplation at 11.30 P.M.	101
Is My Beloved Dead?	103
Soliloquy	105
Futility	106
Meeting Points	107
Helplessness	108
Reflections	109
Amnesia	110

Introspection	111
Inside the Castle	112
Merger	117
Mother's Womb	118
Can I Trust the Lines I Pen?	119
Remembrance of Things Past—	121
History	122
Awesome Being	123
A Cell	124
My Birth	126
Unhappiness	127
Evidence	129
Words	130
A Welcome	132
Nietzsche's Poet	133

Foreword

K. K. Srivastava's third volume of poems, *Shadows of the Real*, is marked by a symmetry and power that I could feel keenly as I read through them over and over again. The poems deal with the contemporary experience, and right away make a sensory response of their own that stays with the reader:

> Here, blindness is notorious.
> We enact a different sense,
> Quizzical looks—
> No answering machines
> The farther we get away
> the more we are replaced
> by what we never intend to represent.

Srivastava's imagination somehow changes the ordinary; his 'world fascinates us, perturbs us/mystifies us,' often reminding us of how necessary it is to recognize and re-examine our perceptions of a world whose horizons we fail to perceive.

This book deserves a large audience. When the poet makes a statement such as 'we borrow our stories from the future,' it only shows his preoccupation with the painful and tender realization of his mind's superior wisdom.

Srivastava's poetry is worthy of our best support. And as in all good poetry, there is something in his poems, a sort of rare grace, which delights and amazes.

15 October 2011   Jayanta Mahapatra

Preface

Poetry: I love to talk of darkness—

1

Sometimes, you admire a thing that lies behind you; you admire yourself for travelling on a road stretching backwards. You go back on the same road, to the same spot, to meet your self-image. What slither out of you are human anomalies unable to dethrone the seized fancies enveloping you. Beneath the burden of such fancies are laid feeble remnants of dreamy, forcibly conceived indeterminate hum that suck so many absorbing voices occasioning you the summit of awakened unrealities. A blind man sees more truth than those gifted with the sharpest of eyes. Poets are like blind people. They find themselves sitting buried in meditation within a strange world, stripped of its own nakedness. Problems of internal and external upheavals, as poets descend into the arena of such a world, being aflame, their conditions can best be described with what Carl Jung wrote: 'How churned up one still is in one's own psyche, and how difficult it is to reach anything approaching a moderate and relatively calm point of view in the midst of one's emotions.'* From total darkness ensues an eddy of a hopeless process; poets indulge into an ever flowing stream—an internal fusion of before and after—going round and round in an illusory circle with no hopes to reach its circumference.

2

Poets write because by doing so they reshape themselves as clouds do in a wind. Writing poems is a way to survive. Poets feel deeply, and those who feel deeply need to survive too. Through life's thorny thickets one searches for a royal road at the end of which one meets a resting place: a fuzzily defined amalgamation of perception, cognition and analysis. A different personality speaks through that great amalgamation. In one magnificent rush, that missing link is arrived at and one sleeps well after innumerable restless nights. Night has depths, one realizes. Writing poems, for me, is tantamount to adventuring on the waters that have not halted at a place, but have been flowing continuously as if there are no obstacles on the way. I often wonder if the journey will be smooth enough to enable me to turn back and ask myself, 'Will you like to tread the same path again?' And the instantaneous answer raises another question: 'What purpose would returning

---

*Carl Jung in 'Essays on Contemporary Events' (1936-1946)

back to the lines I penned long back serve?' It is like visiting the same harlot night after night. I prefer not to waste my nights over over-enjoyed pleasures.'

3

Edgar Allan Poe enchants one with his tales as much as with what he calls trifles. In one such trifle*, he divides the world of mind into the Pure Intellect, Taste, and the Moral Sense: the first concerns with truth, the second with the beautiful, and the third with duty. Try to link these with his tale**, where he prefixes a confounding preface containing narrations as to the relationships between the analytic and the imaginative that go together. So relevant for poets. Poets, if I am permitted to use the terms Poe employs, fond of 'enigmas, of conundrums, hieroglyphics…' use their 'retentive memory' to arrive at a 'sum total of good playing' which has 'the whole air of intuition.' These are here the instincts of the poets who get funereal revelations.

For me a single idea squints at the middle of the night. In the black vigil of despair, I spot a faint beam of happiness. An impossible utopia life seems to be. That idea spills itself into fragmentations—a poem is born. I move from one word to another, from one line to another, in search of a unified whole that lacks unison and cohesion. Life is exactly this; all throughout you

---

*Edgar Allan Poe in *The Poetic Principle*
**Edgar Allan Poe in *The Murders In The Rue Morgue*

seek separate impressions trying to pull themselves into union, unsuccessfully. A poem, like life, regulates itself as much as it constitutes itself. It is akin to employing a gestalt experience i.e. putting feelings, will, thoughts and experiences together to yield place to something that is new, raw and inexperienced. The worst part of any monologue is that the talker only listens. The best part is he only records. Monologists confront them to themselves, to their tragedies, but most importantly they connect; they connect them to others, from their internal depths emerges a prism through which we are all seen standing on the shimmering edge of dualistic connectivity.

4

Writing a poem is like looking at a weird picture, a painting that is so clear as to portray nothing but indistinct images; you see clouds and in their shapes, sometimes you see traces of life and sometimes complete silences of death. You are in bed flooded with anxieties inherited from the past, and also with anxieties you hope to get in future: sandwiched you are with or without sleep. Nights are only nights—some form of light that sheds no light. That is the time I write down my thoughts, I write down my memoirs, I write down pleasures and pains, I write down what I don't want to remember and read; my lines wish to thrive on their multitudinous meanings or versions of one meaning, peripherally glimpsing on its constituent units, nebulously standing afar. You enter the highest and the deepest of insights; and like Descartes you tend to think that there is thinking, and hence, there are thoughts. Poetry is thinking of thoughts; it is about thinking subtleties.

5

It is through Marcel Proust's fascinating but exhausting amplification of what happens in between the last moments of waking state and initial moments of sleeping state: things, ages, memories, remembrances come and go in between as though nothing of any importance is left, that I actualize the art of writing. Writing is as private to me as my desires to spend a few hours with a woman of my choice. Excitements, as a writer, trouble me but never distract me; my creeping into a state of subconscious from the conscious, and an uneasy desire to ultimately and completely melt my conscious into the unconscious is never a strange phenomenon for me. It just happens. I am in a no-man's land, having the liberty that bestows on speculative minds the liberty to move to and fro—a way into innumerable reciprocal causations that ultimately culminate into a world of ideas. 'Shifting and confused gusts of memory', as Proust calls them, function decisively in as much as these delve into linkages between the past and the present. For me analyzing my ideas has never been so easy; I am faced with an inferred state of a heterogeneous whole wherein is transmitted to me a faint, chromatic interaction of the past and the present, and also an array of succession and penetration of moments that has long become part of the past and that seem to be turning towards the present. Memories do fail, I admit and admire.

But these failed memories do not rob my thoughts of their sense and value. I hate to bury a thought. A thought is an uncomfortable evenness or a comfortable unevenness both limping towards the shadow bidding adieu to me. Whatever it is, it is worth my ink. The best poems are born very late in the night when nothing but poets and their ideas stay awake, struggling to shun the first rays of the morning. Poetry is born in the darkling womb of mysteries of mind where intensity of emotions and sensations, though placed on differing footings, influences it as moments continue to flee.

6

I bring myself to a significant question. Are poets 'Rational fools'*, seeking through their poems, a collective rationality to address ethical issues, particularly when they write keeping in mind an audience as helpless as they are? Is their effort worth the excruciating pain they undertake to express their anguish, arguments and affirmation? Is it not the irrationality, the vagueness of issues that renders them utterly senseless—answers are extremely difficult to come by and sometimes these never come; questions become so redundant as to defy any logical answers. Poets hate questions the way they hate human beings who dangle this way or that as situation dictates. For poets, the seductive illusions of dream worlds they create

---

*'Rational Fools' is title of an essay written by Prof. Amartya Sen as published in his book *Choice, Welfare and Measurement*

help them in yelling, 'Everything out there is false.' It is a false world we cherish and rejoice. Intertwined with this false world are the intellectual brutalities of men, obsessed with irrational impulses espousing laudable goals. Like John Nash who came out of schizophrenic torpor while thinking of the dilemmas of the two prisoners who did get no opportunities to meet each other, and thus opted for second best solution, poets too tend to grapple with ethical issues, unable to reach a solution, even the second best. Ethical issues for poets raise conflicts of identity—individual as well as collective—and coupled with infirmity of historicity these ail them the way twins ail each other—having no identity of their own, and a desire to seek separateness but unable to get rid of the other's identity. The simultaneous order of irrevocable sufferings and sorrows imprison the frequent visits to lands of anonymity and speculations, and poets, as prisoners, keep seeking their own identity through their outpourings. These are unknown, inhabited paths poets travel exploring strangeness of worlds that lies just beyond their obvious reality which quarrels with its own realness. Poets sublimate their confessions to some sort of formal images. Multiplicity of subjects—imagined and inferred—a dialogue with what you don't know. Poets sense riddles lying all around, unable to realize the existence of such riddles. Unhinged as these riddles are, they are lost as, Schopenhauer ably avers, amidst the cognitive forms of appearance. They wantonly forsake their ideas and ideals, rapturously seeking a way out. Poets hanker after an identity that is beyond the reach of boundaries of their intuition and imagination. Fabulous hopes of the past don't constitute forlornly desired wishes for the future. Worthies of modern times find trust in untruths and immoral responsibilities that they discharge with a sort of spiritual impulse in which oftentimes we, or almost most of us, perceive a dearth of veracities, a series of hermeneutics of suspicion. Trust—a great but intriguing word that has destroyed so many myths about trust and distrust as well. Rationality in poetry, in modern times, is the first to be pushed to the rough corners of irrationality.

7

A few of my poems are long. Why long poems? How are these different from small ones? How many lives are there in long poems? Is the psyche of a poet fractured in such poems? Various psyches keep battering him as he engages himself in working out the sequencing of the poem. There is unification and there is fragmentation. And in this unification and in this fragmentation, a poet feels one with himself; he comes closer to himself. Relationship between the physical world and the internal one is an open secret here, a complex secret impacting his poems. Streams and streams of people come and leave us; a few make us think of them afterwards. Why? Because they introduce to our psyche, a weightless and motionless murky world of passion and pretence, a profound intervention of high order—an intervention that whistles us out and out, again and again. They, to say in brief, engrave our capacity to judge and, thus, inanities continue. 'Shaping spirit of imagination'*, yes, this is how Coleridge calls judgmental capabilities. The confused mass of thought-provoking issues never help me in distinguishing between the worthy and the worthless. Creation is an outcome; difficult to fathom but true to its core. Creators are veritable fountainheads of stories: an inexhaustible ocean of exquisite and enigmatic tales. A long poem is exactly this.

Poets face their own enigma more so while writing longish ones. They enter the clustering logs, thinking nothing of the log and bring out pieces unfathomably logical. The incessant variation of their thoughts carries with it images impacting the mind capable of dreaming. Particles glimmer, images within images glimmer allowing thought processes a reach into these images within images essential for long poems. The hot cauldron of noisy stars—I mean, our brain and its deeper recesses—differentiates, maybe not so candidly, between unborn ideas and uprooted ideas, deceitfully hiding obsessive impulses. Amidst that weight lies a wait—irreversibly long wait—when they experience thoughts' sterile grounds looming onwards—an intersection they sit since time immemorial, unable to occupy it any longer and also to leave it.

8

Soft and gentle movements are supposed to give us pleasure, so believes Aristippus. Have you ever heard echoes of sound crowded in a man's silence? Silence—

---

*Samuel Taylor Coleridge in 'Dejection: an Ode'

soft and gentle—is never dull. Wrapped in the spell of silence, creatures of stillness sum up the gigantic stories of giants that make history—the muffled and dumb history that weeps over the sagacity of silent spectators. Fame hangs in detours these giants never dare enter, for if they ever enter there, they would simply melt away as would their fame. Nothing damages an individual or even an institution more severely and more gravely than poorly comprehended, hasty, baseless notions and experiences which people believe to be unassailably true and leave no stone unturned in rearing a lofty edifice of untruth on these uncertain, infirm and vague foundations. In making room for deeper purpose, these denizens portray a remarkable kind of abysmal knowledge of their being in stillness of deepening dark from which I see no escape for them. They would keep sinking in the abyss out there, for they share the comfort with their peers. Dark things soothe.

9

A mind which has never nurtured a thought, a cussed case of cerebral inertia, whirls and whirls. So many such minds get together and they turn out to be the most prominent critics of creativity. Their voice resonates. Intellectual disgrace reigns supreme. Spoken words make legends—a guiding philosophy of life for those who go cataclysmic when an outer reality threatens their very trust in untruths and immoral responsibilities, and thereby their flawed substance. They are simply unable to maintain themselves knowing it well they have nothing to transmit

except their well-cocooned fears of facing an outer reality in which they find no validation of their fantasies—jewels among the beads. Notoriously known for their infatuation with their wondrous achievements which make them ponderous, fabulating and confabulating, these creatures wallow in nothing of significance and demur, needlessly, at an outer reality that they perceive as carrying unremitting layers of reflexive critique.

10

I know my limitations. All writers, poets, philosophers, essayists and ilk that I have read have strengthened my limitations: they have not helped me in defining what these are but in perceiving these succinctly. Sometimes perception is dubiously deceptive, crawling within tiny circles, unable to move out. It fails you when you need its help, it tortures you when you need its soothing influence, it suffocates you when you need liberation from it.

This collection enables me to bring to fore reflections that have been passing through my mind: the literary ideas, unclear or ill-formulated experiences, the never-exhausting clash of words with incisive ideas, unsettled gloom that each day brings with it, albeit unintentionally—morbid thoughts hidden beneath melancholic immobility, unique in its splendour, all helping me explore pathways to immense possibilities of reaching out to consciousness of existence, a voyage into the being and the becoming, the world of estrangement and alienation in the backdrop of Pascal's image of man—man with weak body, immensely aware of his stupendous power as a thinking being—of whom Pascal possibly had in mind when he wrote, 'One must have a totally blind mind to be capable of wrong reasoning about principles which are so broad that it is virtually impossible to overlook them.'* Through these poems, I understand the limitations words place on me; words don't help me explain myself fully or my thoughts: blurred and sometimes inexplicable images and scenes, grafted in my fantasy, accrue to reality as if from the edge of an inner world of darkness, I, as a writer, am limping into inners of the world of yet another darkness. Illusions of my past constitute illusions of my present—I visualize these illusions, untrammelled, as I seek refuge to enter into obscurity of another kind. And as I do it, Thoreau's words ring into my ears, 'The light which puts out our eyes is darkness to us. Only that day dawns to which we are awake. There is more day to dawn.'**

11

Dancing with an unknown partner (my poems) is queasy. It is like spotting a black cat in a dark room when the cat is not there. But the room exists, the darkness exists, very much in the world I create and fill with words. The source of creation is inscrutable: it cannot stand in a relationship other than the one with its creator. It is a mirage situated in the mind. My poems represent a concentration of

---

*Quoted by Nirad C. Chaudhuri in *Three Horsemen of the New Apocalypse*
**Henry David Thoreau in *Walden And Other Writings*

expansion—there is no skewing. Like many, I too seek, in my poems, that illuminated spot which makes a poem great but in doing so I am confronted with lacerating interiority of poems. Thus, I round up—the importance of reconciliation of differences of perceptions and attributes not so foreign to you, you climb up to yourself, and then suddenly realize that the ladders are pulled. You grope into the whole from which parts have suddenly disappeared, and like Leibnitz, you begin seeking reality of parts to determine the nature of the real parts of the whole. So is constituted the beauty of a poem. Readers, enjoy the freedom to go athwart.

12

Either/or, Neither/nor—To my gentle, courteous and discerning readers, I am revealed through these poems.

K. K. Srivastava
New Delhi

Our Being Us*

Another day,
on the abysmal continuum
Another surreptitious reflection
neither doubled nor redoubling
of our consciousness, yet another day
and its schematic perceptions
no trembling fixedness, so it seems.
Here, blindness is notorious.
We enact a different sense,
Quizzical looks—
No answering machines
The farther we get away
the more we are replaced
by what we never intend to represent.
We are not perplexed as yet
our fall does not perplex us,
We borrow our stories from future:
Distant one,
Churchy darkness of the past
we manage like visions.

Are we missing something or
there is no question;

---

*I express my gratitude to Romanian poet and writer Veronica Valeanu for her help in refining this long poem.

We feel like sluts,
the truth of it; we are totally slut,
Being directed to a lousy waiting room
knowing not how to cover our wounds.
It is not tied around our neck
We have not wrapped it
Marvelling at worries and wonders
we make ourselves important,
and having reached that limit
share our fascination with the vision
asleep.

~

Wizened with waiting
we are not going
to feel this way again—
The mind crackles in
Unable to silhouette the maze of false
starts and imperfect endings
Death of present desires
invents new ones.
Light dwells upon:
Our shadows look like black,
gigantic boxes on the move,
We survive on indistinguishable surfaces
No perfect mirror displays imperfect expansions
the possibility of our being us
a mere, simple coincidence.
Coincidences,
their multiple-changing fortunes

jumbled, fragmentary stories know
we are alive.
We rarely come upon enigma of permanence
in the gravest recess of our being
Our lives are like that
A sly—a combination of what seems real and
what seems unreal
A mystifying barrier to our being us.
Substance—no real phenomenon
we whirl at unreal happenings,
uncoupling real happenings from unreal realities
flight and escape like irreversible time and reversible space
the gaping holes in our thinking.

~

The world
fascinates us, perturbs us
quizzes us, mystifies us;
This is the use of being placed here
the inner recesses of congealed intensity;
we insightfully beleaguer
unleashed intellect amid
—a sizzling hollowness.
No way to ascertain truths from labyrinth of untruths
dancer from the dance,
no escape route—
Collective mind—the gaze inside the luminous chamber
does not torment
The failing of our senses stays unexplored

Hidden hands play havoc
absurdly and self-defeatingly.
Enchanting echoes of the past
The days we hear of, not seen
our movement,
Drowsy movements hail
the contemplation,
Our being us: a perpetual renewal.

~

Let us weave a web of fragments
scattered all over
it is the 'whole',
that falls, the silent moment
persisting over time.
The continuum—controlled and unrestrained
No explorations, no drifts, no inhibitions
Bodies move weirdly
against the nothingness;
Hopes and grievances pitted against one other
acute fire, inside, outside.
Absences remain uncontained
creations—
absences and presences share ageless roots
Same origin, insecure memories and secure amnesia,
send us back to our beginning.
Where we began
occur no patterned, seemingly illogical cahoots
emptiness galling to its core.
We develop a nostalgia for things

we serve as memorials
Glimpses mean nothing of value
sinking and overtly resurfacing
stories with no eyes, no clues.
Thriving on useless emotions
Memories steeped
what is and what cannot be—
emptied past, spun in
a dizzying blur in time out of time,
holding no hopes for us,
One story becomes all stories—
these soothe and these fail to soothe—
An end.

~

We survive in this one-eyed world,
a clash between memory and memories,
You see a thing
and you don't see a thing,
A child sees the world as a shining sun,
An old man as collapse of all hopes,
neither being nor becoming
secures us an immunity from
either.
A child stays a child just as
an old man an old man,
the one-eyed world repeats
the old, hackneyed story,
there is deeper purpose:
between knowledge and perception

between perception and knowledge
The myth swindles:
the mythical image is one for me
and one for you
We both together measure all our
knowledge and all our perception
a continuous flux—a moving horizon
neither being nor becoming is the same.
The double movements
Appearance of one element
not to be known at all—
for what seems plausible one moment
has its implausibility
next one
What seems to be being now
seems to be becoming next
A fight between truth and falsity
A fight between a puzzle
and its missing parts—
a sense of self-contradiction
deeply embedded into
being and becoming.

~

An unseemly predicament
Inexplicability of lifelong betrayals
A guard and a guide
giving quietus to imperial thoughts
An impasse occurs and recurs
our desires chuck in their hands

Their inherent restlessness
stands out through our blur.
Where will this exploration fix into?
A long thrill in the tunnel
being and becoming—countervailing forces
true to each other
So many things
lying in wait
as if, any moment, uncertainties of
such a moment would start
walking—meditating—thinking
it walks on and on—an invigorating
edge it reaches and then reverts back.
No way..........
You look at your self-effacing ghost
becoming one with one
being one with one
A ghost has more real value.

~

Why it so happens
on certain days
a sense, blacker sense, haunts us
The impurity of small segments
of its existence that we loath,
we say it repeatedly
Still we adore its flattering colours
amid layers of polish
Our itching for its sanctum sanctorum
implies our living near it

and our living far away from it.
There is a hard skin
hiding our being or becoming
you cannot remain in being or becoming
Belief implies possibility of disbelief
Decadence not necessarily an evil
its permanence makes a being a becoming
and a becoming a being.
There lies that improbable state
afloat on the surface
lying beyond our consciousness
in causeless moments
at variance with its image;
That improbable state is not a thought
certainly not,
we love to end up drowning in it.

~

Glaringly unfilled holes in the wall
watch the hours, days, years:
Time unworthy of retrieval
reaches a conclusion—a worthy man
with anaemic eyes,
unable to get over his strangeness,
must let these moments pass,
let nothing be left at cross purposes.
History remembers only those
who, once upon a time, stood still
not bowing their hanged heads to
placid and splendorous contours

of being or becoming.
Obliterate into
a contourless zero, a huge vacuum,
Certain titanic question marks expect
our withering into these
These are ready to renew our existence
Let us forget our scrambled oldness—
movement from old to new
a faint recollection
you only recollect what was in store
Its dormancy reminds us
forgotten being or becoming hides a glimpse
of newness.

~

Drenched in reason
our heights are really plain planes
we creep very slowly
as if fear of our death
brings us so close to it:
Close still hidden behind clouds
of our being
Even the most tiny spot
resembles our being us.
What are we left with?
You will come with arguments
again, arguments—imprinted on our
collective senses:
Don't believe yourself, for you
represent an unbelievable edge of

an abyss
growing into your graveyard.
You compel me.
Can you stand straight and erect?
Riddles you set forth
but tired, malodorous ones
You hate your opponents
but your falling statue must
not reduce you to dust
wherein you embrace your being
incapable of receding itself from
its own becoming.

~

Doubts have details
details doubts
despairing of each other
Knowledge wavers between nothing
we know and everything that we cannot
know—ontological dilemmas;
We feel manifold impulses
that know not us.
It is a pain. It is a pleasure.
Both lie far apart
in the anguish of their togetherness
that chokes
Our impure breath keeps us alive.
We respect our longings
these climb as restless wanderers
coming to the brink of madness

springing out in openness.
An icy thing, a perpetual
enchantment is always alive
within us, without us.
Stop, stop that flying away of your
irrational flux safeguarded in the
ivory tower of your being.
Reality owns everything but in
transmuted form;
Another day swings between
trauma of being and
greater trauma of becoming;
In between we journey into
fragility of dreamless sleep: life.

~

We seem to believe,
nothing that exists chagrins us
nor what does not,
We trust untenable parts;
the wholeness of us,
hunts the being down.
In the larger disquisition
the whole image is
embedding the glimmers of
the unconnected,
of interdependency and reciprocity.
An insight opens and escalates.
Led astray,
disillusioned against our

expectations,
a vain challenge to the void,
no future, no past and no memory
overtakes us.
We appear in the midst of unfolding
distances, condensed in a single being
spread across all inevitabilities
of being or becoming.
A form?
An appearance?
Indeterminacy
of either or both?
One comes out of one's
otherness, you move
yet you see no motion; it is
but a motion, it stands still,
it exists; seen and used,
its outside is its inside.
Our senses roam everywhere,
the pure past of experiences
a surpassed and unvisited past
holds a promise; a disordered
being would be realized soon.

~

The insane darkness
descends in the capes of their forms
and hums a story
a story of a painter's job,
a man's face, a desolate and distraught

face emerges out of the quagmire
of lifeless efforts at becoming.
An awakened desire
comes with a simple wish:
'I would seize the past
And I would seize the future.'
Between the past and the future
lie the dreams that desert the being
the dreams that persist with the becoming.
Self-created revelations;
we rise again in search of
'I' of being and 'I' of becoming.
Innumerable waves
hazily staring at us and
the stretched shades of infinite traces, vast
we walk all again a long, lonely jungle;
Lengthened rhythms of past
can never be reborn, alas.

~

Life's dreariness
steps on to the lower
plane of reality:
anything but an expression
of hidden feelings, dredged
up in broken delusions
staying, unexplored,
A relationship between
antiquity and contemporaneity.
An impalpable greyness

a trepid, formless content
an unreflecting opacity
an awful mystery
await the return of the being
to the becoming.
Amid doubts and conflicts
the soul becomes maimed
irresolute—naively seeking truth
between appearance and reality;
Rare glimpse of life
manifestation of emotions
going beyond time.
A stranger asks questions…
none answers;
the stranger moves forward
on a road beguilingly meaningless.

~

There seems to exist
a context;
in the very dead of itself
imposing exclusion, a denial
a non-seeing—
a collocation of a void
that awaits, and a fullness
that departs
a sense of
the double world
a form of quest
a lost echo

repeats itself
in sustained reflection
of solitude, vastness and
disdain.
Who welcomes us there?
An anguished awareness
or an enigmatic irrationality
or a treacherous self
or a mixture of all three;
A self-knowledge evades itself
as if a mirror does all jobs but
mirror.

~

In a disconnected mind
comes the perpetually
evolving state of beginning
not stopped as yet,
the beginning begins
We grow old: a meeting point
knocks at our door, quite often
sensing our dreamless slumber
a mirage chased:
Life and death a mingled
passage, a dirge unsung
moves into oblivion from
the burden of consciousness
in search of inexorable wails of pains.
Irrevocable choices of life
reach us to inaccessible

arena: hopeless death blinds
and blinds; life rescues not from
the failure of belief.
A way of seeing the anguished
meaning in the futility of its
making, in that inevitable
circle all envisaged relations
get oriented.

Endowed with inertia
the existence of being
an exteriority to itself
revealed to us; a hollow
upsurge of annihilation
of clogged, viscous
becoming.

~

Pain,
neither absent nor
unconscious, a part of
a distance-less existence
a total grasp with no point
of view—
A permanent fixture
overflowing itself
a co-presence, with an
unseen past:
an inverted vision is nothing
but nothing,

emptied everywhereness
is what—if not silence
incomprehensible.
In that deep-sleeping,
someone seems to be
rolling over;
in dream's churned turbidity
Magnanimous hands
knock at the baffling
bottom of our shores: a parallel
universe, hidden darkness of the
sleep sucks off the unobtainable.
This immobility,
a motion toward a motionless
past-being;
A melodic rhythm,
a reflective consciousness
lurks.

That Night

That night,
melodic whisper of silence,
My eyes, heavily lidded
by overweight of
frozen memories: curly
passions,
unsheltered,
watch near the fringe.

Some nights are so bright,
some so lonesome
The lonely image of that
faceless woman
jewellery of blossoms
walks on; unconcerned.

That night,
waxing moon
wriggles into the night air,
stars stare blankly,
that faceless woman's dark eyes
display mischievous
verisimilitude on night's visage.
Lonesomeness, sometimes
so intriguing.

There are moments
memories suckle at my heart,
That faceless woman reaches
my soul, deep into my soul
within the very core
of me.

That night
in each of my eyes
a little darkness
rolls through the ruins
the faceless woman
leaves inside mine;
I gather abundance of life;
night's lonesomeness,
faintly alive,
drifts lifelessly.

Stray Thoughts

1

Loveliness,
lips aglow
blend in harmony.

2

Spiralling up,
lake of memories,
night's tyranny imminent.

3

On the ochre earth,
scintillating tranquility
stretches lazily.

4

Mirror pours out her beauty,
twinkling in her eyes,
rare music flows variously.

5

Another lonely soul,
stars shining brightly,
what goes never comes back.

6

Ecstatic mind cajoles
twilight thoughts work
by unhinging of logic.

7

Sadness chills his heart,
lightless eyes whisper,
deceitful inevitables grumble.

8

Indefinable cosmic stuff,
the eternal paradox sinks,
horizons submerge in the waves.

9

A single moment,
shields of emotions muted,
life's mystery at bay.

10

Soaked in dampness,
evening lies naked,
subtle treasures stay virgin.

11

Vulnerable truth,
seeks a new voice,
life's call again: we wait.

12

Everlasting culmination,
our sobering thoughts
swim into future's vacuum.

Between Night and Morning

Hang heavily
leftovers of
hardened hours;
Night has just left me
morning wears an unwashed dress.

I made an effort
through camouflaged quagmires
of byways—dimensionless,
these shrivel
carrying a fixed surface
intrusive, everywhere.

Sometimes the hours past swear
to its abandoned failures
purloined treasures
have inherited
magnificent questions
dredged from such failures.

I walk together
with these hours
ahead of me, I wonder
when I will occupy the space
you vacate
and morning will wear a new dress.

Fate

Fate opened
so many doors before me
Looking at each one
I found a loser limping
thoughtlessly away from me.

I have not known
the meaning of victory
A victor succumbs to fate
just as one succumbs
to the folly of twisted wisdom.

Fate
holds its empty burdens;
alive to its slackening wings
light melts with its
shadows; half-roused.

Murkier fate
teaches me
don't bury your dead
climb up to yourself;
to ascend where stars never visit.

Time's Emptiness

Pozzo: 'One day, is that not enough for you, one day he went dumb, one day I went blind, one day we'll go deaf, one day we were born, one day we shall die, the same day, the same second, is that not enough for you?'*

Time:
multifarious oasis
arrayed shoals of happiness
myriad cascades of gloom
holding the universe in place,
and descending
passively
to answer the glories of the
heavens unseen and
hungered pleasures of the earth
unmet.
Successive moments
we remember, not the end.

Futile ashes of
crawling recollections
we dig but in vain.
Questions
of your stillness

---

*Samuel Beckett in *Waiting For Godot*

visit us through your imagination;
hiss of your silence
embodying the living past
vibrates quaveringly.

Beyond you
there is no world,
no givers, no takers
we kneel.

Eternal cycle—
hurled down from your fleeting
cauldron,
No permanent
friends or foes in your cycle;
Against ceaseless odds are pitted
vague symbols
a promise arising from swamps
of your invincibility.

Closed window—
enforced existence,
hallucinatory terrain of
melancholy and mania
gloom and pathos
assurance and elegance
of coexistence
oldness of the known
newness of the unknown:
forms keep changing.

Movements
part of your emptiness
we love to fear you, your might;
the notion—you exist
makes us
grow beyond all
words can describe.
A fear in an idea
an unavoidable idea—
evoking joy, sorrow, desire
aversion, shame and escape
your huge, gigantic abyss:
we succumb to
your looming presence.

A lid of frost
seals your identity,
you have lived here, there, everywhere
sightlessly rejoicing your divine gaze;
Your owlish glasses
explain you can't take back
kaleidoscopic bequeathals.
Swathed in secrets
lost among innumerable mirrors
you move languidly.

Dreaming a dream is not foretelling it—
past's wisdom is no remedy
for future's malady
Sighs that once were

wouldn't get abolished
An unknown nymph guards us.
Is it an endless wait
a fruitless bliss
an endless bliss
a fruitless wait?
Do you represent all—?
In you
we see meaningful
lastness: a frenzied inaction
of perpetual collapse.

Lachrymal memory—
forlorn hopes
alien in guise
hang.
An uneasy retrieval of
broken images, sterile associations
forgotten selves
sinks deep into
fury of your hidden ruins.

An immeasurable gulf
yawns in solitary hearts,
Dwindling disillusionments
have drooped further
These drooped time and again and
countless times
the melody of this moment
is the melody of restless past,

mediating future
the seeker and the sought
hail you.

An infinite living force
your stillness moves everything else
your stillness stands still—a rock that
never moves,
a sublime rapture.
A sadistic acumen persists
marooned by feral dreams
never witnessed earlier
A destroyer visits mankind
sapping its most fearful energies—
architects/engineers of humanity.

A heartless, unpredictable,
unseen, abstract entity
flowing ruthlessly
it is nothing but self-overcoming
through you there exists
a coexistence
a tangle
of unwalked alleys—
reaching us higher than reason
masked,
A mercilessly imprudent mask,
an awful awareness of
commingled realities and dreams
refusing each other.

Inflamed
tranquility sudden, vast,
candescent:
moves quicker and quicker
Antiquity—the language of a noiseless
stream—that hypnotic lining;
feeds clues to
illusory forms.
Our unmemorable past
often circles around completely,
lording over
mummified memories
brightness outside
hobnobs with darkness inside
we don't seek ourselves;
we live nearby.

Paths—
indecipherable signs
seemingly consent to the
dishevelled edges of time,
receding, whirling and returning
thoughtlessly.
A light beyond veil
is no assurance
There are more ways than one
to enter emptiness of the
end of the world.

In the heuristic dream world,
suffused in shimmering wholeness,
your concealed ecstasy
holds aloft.
In the rough sands of life
action stirs dream
dream stirs action
like
passion stirs desire
desire stirs passion—
indecipherable yearnings
disburden.

Time,
wait,
impenetrable quietness
unable to see anything
or absence of nothing;
caught in the currents of time
we curse the art of seeing/feeling.
Sagacious time—a hollow survivor
bright darkness
overpowers us; an idea of
separation,
clumsy and shuffling;
Consciousness rips apart
the dissolving streams of
infinitum.
The wait continues…

In that dark chamber,
in our mind
there are ceaseless knocks:
A sense of shifting
time reverts back
hanging around like
tiny stars in sky
scripted for eternity.
Time leads us,
a glow remains
an endless time remains
A solitary soul comes time
and again,
to weigh man's inner change
imprisoned in the flame
of its disillusionment.

Time, its antics.
In its antics
trapped are we, surviving the same moment;
fulfilling life
exalted through death
raging with echoes of desire.
Events come and go
heading us to
penumbra of darkness
that opens and that closes
peeping through
itself.

Brevity of
human existence
All a game
it is misty, hazy,
nebulous, incomplete
a man exists,
but in futility of his existence
his shadow serves his opposite
his shadow and he have been
through each other,
a game whirls over.
An interpreter
seeks to look and feel inside
a self-introspection
that quivers incessantly,
sinking into a deluge;
Absurdities
of time
benignly survive
the frills of time,
ebbing.

Blindness

Do you need to tell the world
you exist?
Your existence sends no happy dreams
nor does it cause any suffocation,
the world does not need you.

Don't go after purposeless eyes
the vision in these eyes surrendered
long back; much before you came
your existence serves no purpose
to visionless eyes.

Do you need
non-existence—a meaninglessness?
non-existence or an existence
full of meaninglessness
what you want—decide that first.

Silence, absence
in your existence mean nothing
absolutely nothing to eyes blind;
blindness decides you exist or not—
you keep shackling falseness of eyes.

In that abandoned corner
thinking of blindness's cruelty
you suddenly realize,
lonely stars twinkle too
in a rubble of ruins.

Chanakya Puri of New Delhi

Comes the morning,
there occurs the birth:
darkness is born
lit by shadow of its worth.

Towards the evening,
day longs to disappear
in the lawns of my house,
I sit alone, all by myself
a crow caws casually
a small lizard escapes.

In the Nehru park
I see her again, lost to herself
face, partly covered
with dark, very dark hair:
freshness of elusive beauty
dawns.

In the maddening crowd
of Sarojini Nagar market,
A small boy plays by himself
He begs to steal from his childhood,
his life.

In the vegetable market,
cars come and go,

an old hawker's eyes
have hopes rekindled.

7 p.m. everyday
that old, lanky, bearded man
limps along, broodingly,
the headless world has lost all its
meanings for him.

The curvy woman giggles
on mobile—
her dog, nay her two dogs,
her shadows; follow her silently,
an incurable sense
pervades.

They walk, trying to
pass from their body
and onward; unaware, they
drift right
into the lap of night.

A foggy, freezing morning—
in the thicket,
wakes up a chirping lone bird
the doorbell rings
maid-servant arrives.

In the Nehru Park,
two beloveds,
like two unmet fantasies
enjoy their intense embrace

and never-ending kiss.
In the Saheb's lawn
grass are tender and green,
first kisses not far away,
Madam would soon walk over.

that anglicized, bearded
brown Saheb,
steps out of his official car;
murmurs in English
tiny dog wails tail,
dismissively.

Reflection
of the sunset
glows
in the club;
night on the move.

A daily wager
counts his earnings;
His lost poem
seems to have slept
into his fragile eyes.

They are all well-fed
they have no complaints
they enjoy winter in summer
summer in winter;
they decide poverty-lines.

Empire
dark, quite and unshakable
it gives us songs
that have no note of
compassion, have no thoughts.

Tall, green trees
curl up in chilling cold,
The whole night the mother
felt the heaviness of air
Wee-hours,
her child is dead.

A blind beggar
her drooping breasts
hungry child in her lap.

Into the plow
of nothingness
that lady paints a picture
of a light and of a sound
that come and go.

A future is created
out of past observed
life wobbles on; blinded
they stand beside it—
unable to feel it.

An Insomniac's Dilemma

Once again
night has arrived
another chance
to drown myself
into my wakefulness.

These hours
I cannot swallow
nor these can swallow
me—
insomnia is what it is.

Darkness fails
my sleep, ablaze with
its fencelessness,
lets darkness spread
and it meets it there, in exile.

The moon grows
bigger and bigger
My eyelids drift through
their trial of desolation
reaching nowhere.

Are these hours
to flee into deep wells?

Sins

In the heart of night
my sins bleed,
in any dream
things last but against a blank
desire to dream—never blotted out.

I share your anguish
and I drink your tears;
Vagueness of the face unravels
on a desert island
a promise made
doors will be unlocked one day.

I feel it and I know it,
night replete with aromas
frees me of all my sins
in the whore's breasts
I drown in incredible pleasure.

It burns but only for an instant
then it leaves.

Mental Asylum and Poetry

In facing life
one faces death too.
War of
instincts within
madness
on a jagged path
illumined by iridescent
light of intellectual apogee.
Elizabeth Bishop,
Sylvia Plath,
Eliot or Pound,
Poe or one of consequence,
good poetry
is all about
ruminations: pure and simple
deep thoughts revolving
around life's agility,
evolved over
infinity's futility
in mental asylum.

A Doubt

I wander
in strange places
none has visited.
The ageing arms of insolent stranger
grow fainter and fainter.

Living in opaque heights
arms try to reach out to
defenseless sky;
in search of answers
mute questions hover around.

Every question
is a doubt;
as is every answer
just as waking is sleeping
and sleeping, waking.

Life like death—
a mere task of vanishing,
wearing dark glasses,
these never vanish together
but roll through like dreams
in a barrel.

A Mirror

A decision
we would wear dress of snow,
a spotless dress
to curb darkness
blinds us.

One day,
we would rise
from the dead
thinking another applause,
bereft of soul,
welcomes us.

Benevolent days
like nights
refuse to be our shimmering
tombs.
We stand puzzled
like a falling leaf.

Our present shadows
look awkwardly at
their counterparts;
memories of past:
a frivolous mirage.

Our squeezed existence,
tired of multitudinous dilemmas,
in an imaginary world,
A transparent mirror hangs,
One day we will knock at ourselves.

We survive in mirrors
having lived beyond oblivion.

Nothing Left to Tell

My poems reveal me
no longer,
Diverse voices percolate
leaving
unsettled identities.

These identities give me
words whose skin
I break and feel
The kaleidoscopic mind's
poverty of language.

I don't feel strolling dreamlessly
through the tyrannical edges,
some crazy, wild, furious
guys may rip, split my legacy.

Through my poems,
I dare stepping out to
occupy my place
amid nascent hugeness.

A thick veil,
a speck in the void,
miscellaneous rubbish,
these crazy, wild, furious guys.

Muses have grown
autistic,
My poems have nothing
to tell,
Nothing left to tell;
Identities keep
fluttering around.

A Beggar

6 p.m,
Sadness on its back
makes us
irrelevant—indifferent
heaving through
unvanquished irony
unable to chagrin us.
Rooflessness;
His greatest shelter
breaks into pieces.
In his death,
these would reassemble
and humanity would
make discoveries.

Contemplation

Contemplation
Zenith in an intelligent man's
head;
The muse of an inconceivable world
the realization—
Something is always afoot
knocks at the door.
Abundance searches within him
the murderer—the entity
who asks this question—
'Can you confess wrong
without losing rightness?'*
Answers
(my esteemed peers, a plausibility)
disappear back to where
these came from.
Idle questions' wretchedness
fulfills his moments; his joys, his sorrows—
Inconsequential ones
representing elegiac pathos of
his contemplation:
He feels like contemplating
It hiccups.

---

*An analogy with Pound's 'To confess wrong without losing rightness' in CANTO CXVI

Faces

In the midst
this place is no joy;
Open to opposing possibilities;
essential or accidental
Choosing what not to choose.

Faces: fused pasture of
unshaped light,
Ever willing to immerse
in the dizzy acts of desiring
world, it behaves in accordance
with its nature.

That way we have learnt,
the art of surviving/thriving
on facial expressions
substituting the opposite for the original
and vice versa.

Our great strength;
The still-life faces like
skulls without jaws
concealing deceitful jades in
glamorous roles.

We time placements just as
we place timings;
We are hung comfortably on the
right side of wrong tracks
and vice versa.

A new voice will
speak your mind,
A half-illumined, half-obscured
voice will wear new clothes.

Mind

Mind, no colours,
A weasel word,
Its collapsing lips
sleep, at times, wake up, sometimes,
We return to its smoky bars,
An inexhaustible painting waits.
On a whim, you come here
and on a whim you leave;
Piercing brightness,
sanguinary darkness,
enduring decay
drain us.

Mind,
an amorphous collection
of ruined realities,
half-thought dreams,
What has become of everything
these come and go,
kaleidoscopically.
A humdrum world;
Maps the world with scars
creating clean, vibrant history.

A wild river loosens
at your pools

Like its warbling waters
you have no nerves.
Pushed aside
visible all the time;
A surfeit of seeming
slumps forward to invite us.

We turn around slowly
and see silhouettes
eroding slyly; heavy clouds
droop intentionally.

What leaves us?
It is nothing, it is nothing
Your remains are your remains
that walk in front of us.
Let this walk be over
Then we would dwell on
till posterity.

Decisions

Moments linger,
Life continues;
Rotting archive drops
remnants of a labouring
profile; an absent story
filtering lucidly,
Decisions stand awaited.

Living
in dimensions different,
decisions lure us
deeper and deeper
into greater wait,
Incomplete decisions churn.

Unreal stars
on a dismal plain
An ineluctable explanation
hangs unfastened from
their hooks.

Decisions have muteness,
Hopeless convolutions
idiotic silence;
We don't understand this world
despite these brave words,
written/spoken.

Awake and restless
Fear of being entombed alive
robs us of
our self-worth.

Long after we have
ceased to live,
decision still sag
We all stand in awe
looking forlornly;
Indistinct shadows
overwhelm us.

A Day

A day gives you
an answer
but no questions—
Propositions don't matter then.
The day is like
a rain coming in drops
insufficient enough to swim/sink.
This irritation-free day;
You pause as if a great
thought has flashed your
mind,
and you crumble away with
this great thought.
It is a day you
illustrate your ignorance
along with yourself or
alongside yourself,
The day has an inexplicable coldness;
Don't make a life for yourself,
life's splendour lies not in its wait
but in its enigmatic contours.
Inner plights,
wade through wantonly
Its long, suffocating wait,
as the day yields its true
meaning.

A Thought

In the cusp of continued paradoxes,
in a swarm of eyes,
wanton themes shape up:
like cumulus clouds
frequenting our brain.

Lulled, self-bracketed,
into magical thinking,
Reality skin-deep
Eyes; self-involved eyes
blind to myriad relations
otherwise visible,
Surfaces reveal,
deceive too.

An indefinable step,
seeks occasions to see
the paths ushering us
nowhere.
A bonny morning
Hidden parts
dragged by migratory urge
dislodge.

Thoughts
divorced from imaginative

trust,
in broken voices
getting inshape
like a subtle illness.

Something grows inside us
We keep waiting for ourselves.

Hopes

Hopes,
search of promise,
winds make.

Trickling down
sands of time
roil.

Long afternoons
nothingness
deep calm follows.

Milky haze
lingering, far off,
shrouded mountains,

Before your birth
you are lost,
flying in parallel lines,

Posthumous existence
lasts, hinged on
unswayable.

Success

Questions present.......... once again:
Will I ever reach the end of this thin, long rope?
After a certain stage questions make no sense,
Anfractuous, silent questions, their currents so low,
falling into the mire, drowned answers float back;
uncertain if these would remain the same.
To fill empty shelves I listen to soft, precious moments,
infected thoughts I would have to penetrate through,
My mantel of iniquities pleading warmly with me,
as if this thin, long rope perfects its jerkiness.
When I see people hiding themselves behind the
the prism of their forked smile,
their body and mind broken, shattered and shaking,
and stepping onto others to steal eminence,
relishing the imperfections of their dignity, honesty
I judge the tenderness of moments; their faceless presence
vowing I would never reach the end of the thin, long rope.
It is an intriguing rope, full of myths and mysteries,
black crows in the sky have started descending
towards the earth; rainbows in the sky have started shedding their colours,
someone would go soon,
the striker in heaven strikes at the right moment,

the harsh beauty of death we all drink from the clay mug.
In assessing desperation through the hopes, standing by,
our search for meaning of life, reachable/elusive,
a guiding light, an old, chilling refrain , succumbing to the very shadows we have been holding onto, lamenting the wisps of unfulfilled bliss.

Whispers

Mind
lightless chamber
dreams.

Woman
coloured rose
heavenly bliss.

Tranquility
disequilibrium
poem.

Senility
busy bodies
success.

Day
collapses
night.

Image
unimaginable
modern art.

Space
uninhabited
loneliness.

Distress
rejoice
rescue.

Love is Not Deception

You—an enigmatic mirror,
Frigid and blustering restlessness
reaches for me again,
I see you once more in your stillness,
making out what secrets lie in you.
It is you who has stood beside me all along
disguising yourself, trailing the dusts of my dreams
Hopeless pain of being unsighted;
Another emotional drowning
washes away heavenly togetherness.
I never did misprision you, you
like life beneath the turbulent sea
like a mysterious whistling breeze
like the gathering calm of the desert,
an instant answer flits over all impalpabilities.
I have left the cloudy realities behind,
forgotten the filthy, torturing memories—
Invincibility of the
vast vicissitudes of life.
All exits and all entrances
In some chancel of my psyche,
The abyss of my dismal mind
copes with ecstatic mellowness.
In the white cauldron of anguish,
I never cease to look at the star-swept sky,
Knobs of sound curl up from the cold,

Wakeful days would never be restored.
You invisibly unfold those uneasy dreams
that exist but only for you,
I, a lonely refugee,
see wilderness rising and sprawling around
Still I treasure those significant moments
treasuring those significant moments,
love is no deception.

Voids

Voids;
Soundless,
we escape there
to avoid anarchy
of naked, lifeless,
frothing euphoria
looming up in our
limping mind.
Voids
struck into being by
diminution of illegible
failed substance
to measure voids.
In a luxury of
fond embrace:
we take a pledge, we
get rid
of these voids.
Then,
we come across
patterns we fail to order
into meaning.
We find it difficult to
trust and believe
being in the graveyard
of feigning voids—
Resemblance of the
clothesline of realities.

Lonely Travellers Go Astray

Lonely travellers wallow in
unsettling dilemmas
Hidden facets of theirs
stand beside them,
Something else everywhere
like a silent volcano,
about to enter
their silence.

Only solitary companion
moves incessantly
like a single drop
in an traversing river;
lonely travellers go astray.

Every drop a great dilemma
Deserts don't have mirages;
No whirlpools in mighty rivers;
Unknown trees send aroma
of their gravity.

In deep introspection,
humming the tune of
the melody's ultimate
destiny, life is putrid, filled
with ennui.

Everything, someday,
sometime becomes standstill,
in a lampless cell
Everything, someday,
comes to a halt, a standstill,
establishing their equation
with time.

Faultlessly,
a new day arrives at
night's experiences go away,
Brooding eyes once again look at
these travellers as if mirages, whirlpools,
Unknown trees don't exist;
curtly moving into
oblivion,
like lonely travellers
never seek emanations.

Fog

Pale shades of the evening;
the colourful shyness of rainbow,
plethora of dreams come together
fog has just emerged
from the anfractuous empire of clouds.

Sealed Remembrance

This moment not immune from your thoughts;
my delusional woes stirred,
kissing crowning aspirations of
ethereal skies;
bushes of harmonies
the effervescent
laces of my musing lyrics.
My defenses innocently let
the inner blaze loose upon
the chalice of imagery;
Ebbs of a melancholic mind induce
thoughts disarrayed.
I am permitted into a quiet reservoir
of omitted memories.
Sometimes our lunacies are our brightest spots
Every pathway its own stories to tell
Stories like shackled hands
spreading out in the veins of mute
unmoving memories.
Your very immutable marks
you gave me words
and you gave me what never stay
behind these words: their hollowness.
You promised me a new world
Where is that world?
Let me discover that new world

ever ascending world
slipping out of my hands.
Your thoughts are glamorous thoughts
immune by themselves
not felt outside
There dissolve all boundaries,
all cultures, all dreams
It is here I search you
life really so colourful.
Your loitering in foggy mirror
broken images or split images
no true reflections.
If at all I go
without the invigorating wine
of your thoughts
I would be left with you
neither fully flared
nor fully blown out—
Greatest tyranny of the remembrance
you sealed for me.
My eyes have learnt a difficult lesson
shun other eyes in the night,
in the dimmed rays,
on the light-laddered waves
You travel alone in that intense form
welcomed by caged alienation.

From Within

From within
stretches out a numbed belief,
Dormant calm resurfaces;
The frail visage of merciless
faith,
sways gently in the wind.

From within
we are led nowhere
all signs obliterated;
faded babbling utterances
reach the other side of
meaning.

From within
lazy contours scream
as if a tiny boat vying
with itself, unsuccessfully,
on a howling, furious
sea.

From within
the dim twilight thickens
full and mighty dawn shrinks;
the anguish of separation
the defenses of voiceless pangs
wasted away.

From within
the pageant of pagan glory
enduring its torments;
Nothing else would be lost
struggling waits yearn for
the lip's first touch.

From within
waves of forgotten horizons
look for invisible anchors;
Spilling moments, languid eternity,
yet another wet world of dreams
melts away.

Image of Life

Leaning back,
let us sense
the image of life,
Another extension
of death.

~

The image and its
extended image
meet and cling,
Brittle, dry mirror
breaks.

~

Once, a
reason,
now, a confluence
of several evasions,
fed on deception of oneness.

~

We hear the
inconsequential muse,
antique noises, numberless,
emptied, aborted eyes,
The wave decides: divides.

The divine innocence,
Clouds come near and go far,
The inexplicable mystery,
not a mere accident: both
leaping in each other's arms.

Through Time

Sitting at the edge,
weird darkness
explores benign
existence,
We see ourselves in light.

~

Everyone understands,
grievous songs:
travails of lost memories,
ambered by time,
We relish our invisibility.

~

Unhealed impressions,
Life—a mirror reconstructed,
In between balance and
proportion lies
our kaleidoscopic visibility.

~

Ethereal sentience
every vision, a revision,
a waking dream
drops into stagnant duration,
absences in life—too anguishing.

Let us long for the nameless,
besieged by thinning days,
What is there that knocks;
an awful awareness,
it takes nothing to balance.

A Sketch Made in December

Winter's
primitive silence,
Vast space of
jewelled asymmetries
unrolls;
No end in sight.
A Castle—
an attempt to fill
numbing outlines,
an incorrigible breeze
passes by so very close.
This vastness cannot
devour another;
Lonely lamp listens and waits,
looks bemusedly
at the cold, hard world.
A figure contains
many more figures,
Confusion blinds
the perception.
Sketch refuses,
it reflects on past
For it,
future has no value.
Doors and windows
hide scattered stories

No matter where the
picture hangs now.
Tall, dead trees
longing for time to pass
Yes. Who are they
without you?
Sketch unlocks
deep, irretrievable fears;
enclosed by time
Perhaps these will
break loose—a sketch.

Depression

Darkness outside
Nothing has changed
neither the source
nor the expectation.
Out of formlessness
it shuffles forward
invisibly,
I thought it had died;
It, alive—wavering
in its cabin.
This dense night;
my childhood lays
itself bare,
once again.
Floating freely
the same, known fire
burns me inside:
I have no proof of
my innocence.

A Woman

Flaws
Still I owe you a debt
Relation a worthy gift
Let us look into the rift
Your perfection makes you a…woman.

How many times I can run away
Reason not lovelier than thee
Knowledge not loftier than thee
Penetrating you not a diversion
You rise—
a higher, culminating stage.

Your eyes move,
freak me out
What is so immoral
in my longing for your hips
or in my kiss lingering on your lips.

Searching the truth
behind throttled dreams,
Life's celebrations at dizzy zeniths;
There heave in torridity
mute memories.

Breasts,
pristine peaks of purity
eternal realm of resplendence
vicissitudes of solace
bringing life to me and me to life.

Unmarred pearls
Splintered mirrors
look back at you
Ecstatic bliss
unwalked dream.

I probe an infinitude
The silence of crescent,
the exile of your existence
Between the night and the morning
love interferes with depths.

The wind outside hears
what transpires inside
within the boundaries of night
From what reveals what
emerges this poem.

Afternoon Musings

Sitting idle,
That afternoon sun shying away, slyly
Shadows walking off slowly
waiting for the night to subsume
equally idle
Bee buzzes in my ears: life grows.

Thinking of times
I would be old enough to be young
(I wonder why only in afternoons, I think so).
Furtively stealing the glimpses of youth
I realize the youth is wounded
This moment's passion haunts it.

Youth and old age
like next-door neighbours shunning each other
The two neighbours love not each other
(I wonder could Bible be so wrong?)
The whole of my life is no division
at either shore I feel no revision.

Human Illusions

One wonderful day,
after many years of misery
A double guise—
guiding our steps,
meander by meander
waiting for the fate
to arise at an anointed place.
Marked by scars
lovelessness implies
one meets oneself in deep abyss.
Familiar roads seem to have become
labyrinths
That wonderful day weighs upon
us—a cruel rock has come our way.

~

Our fruitless travels
like old wrinkled yearnings;
Complications of existence
bloom and spread
with no colours of our own,
We go ahead painting a random image.
Robbed of real meanings
we embrace
pathways affirming our faith
in imminence of collapse;

Murkier revulsion
lords over awkwardness
of our nakedness.

~

A voice collapses.
Innocent dreams
of a voice;
Deafness:
Absurdity of creation.
Human illusions,
full of unanswerable questions
inadequately, inanely poised.
A part of that illusion
partly opaque;
obviousness, gruelling
as if a king roams around under
the dark shadows of his unmet dreams
the spectrum blazes.
Ambivalence's greatest enemy—
the shreds of rudimentary logics,
move adrift on giant strides
accompanied by the faint blare
of cursed ambitions.

~

There is an order, a method
we cannot live outside;
Fed on sequestered thresholds
drunken pen

Captures its cruelty
madness of the poet, distinct
and jarring
Whisks him to words
lips of ink aspire to kiss.

~

Amid the stress of midnight
we leave behind the islands
off our shores
Within the flowing crevice
of futility of walls
there are no shades
we can relax and muse.
Certainty of the end
no uncertainties about it
Sunken notions
the lower and the higher
meet in a dead chamber.
Omnipotence of our wishful thinking:
Redundant images
embrace each other.

~

A passion,
a la Henri Bergson*
A progressed form of
deep but faint desire
as if childhood

---

*Henri Bergson in *Time and Free Will*

has sprung back
in forms and in shapes
multitude.
Limbs,
paralyzed limbs
Nevertheless we run and we run
so distinctly
so cleverly: winning is nothing
but a feeling of effort.
A wise man has choices
his will—free and undisputed.

~

Unceasingly stilled,
lonely music of resplendent illusions
a desert of vociferation,
Evil leads to good and good to evils
An infinitude opens its doors
We are left to the walls:
unknown forms of the walls.
Illusions,
their grainy images
visioning their un-self
that plays with its echo.
Let illusions pass through
the filter of our morbidity
We continue
unable to cope with the verisimilitudes
of reality.

~

Breathing beneath us
a hundred winds scour
logic ceases in sense.
The house is ruined;
Zones of lucid light
spread all over
an unsure road.
Our wait for broken kisses
rocks us hard:
A heartless luxury grips us.
There are changes and changes
Within a change a smaller change
One change does not alter
another change
Life swallowed by illusions.

~

The unsightable, sighted
The enduring tells a lot about us;
Our intentions: pure and ethical
as the butcher's knife
used skillfully on a sacrificial goat.
Glance aside
oftentimes
Glancing aside does wonders—
it gives us a life of
ease and splendour amidst
multitudes of clouds gathering
amidst the setting sun.

~

A force—a unified force
outside of its body
floats on a phantom reservoir.
It vies with its inertia
Partings get hardened in white space
Beyond death you go no further
Dryness and darkness
keep thrashing our thoughts
Whirled in a tangle
its tight-lipped mouth.

~

Heavenly vice and hellish virtue
Happiness of being able
to be one with both
Hysterical benignness
comes out with another incoherence.
We are thrust in among the lost ones.
In the middle of the night
as our fragments disunite
we welcome the eerie furies of illusions
quietly prolonging their hoary stiffness.
To the dreamy heights
to the shrouds of misty shadows
to the vibrancy of unleashed reality
we succumb ultimately;
A natural corollary of waves of illusions.

~

Little by little
the deep-seated passions

raise their head against
various colours of spectrum,
The contrast seems incongruous
imbued in the quagmire of
slippery revulsions.
Light of intuition
passing over into itself,
the final act yet to be over
we consume our life
learning about our antecedents.
Two final actions:
confused recollections
reign supreme.

~

Our illusions
lead us on
our huge wings.
Standing in the middle,
a piece of dust makes
us feel safer: another
subdivision unrelents.
It happens
and it happens again
Unread are the meanings in
the historical disassociation;
temptable remains our
jewelled stupidity.

~

Waves of illusions;
ocean of their vacuum
Things are so clean
needing no purity,
Devils—
helping us meditate
our words of wisdom
never fall on the ground.
What allures us—
the unified entity
of a separate life
engulfed by unfamiliar routes,
An ever-interrupted reality
of hopes/despair stand erect.

~

We stay unhurt,
Unclad illusions—
vacuums, devoid of possibilities
We have failed again, once again
to heed to the essence of illusions
we slip into the lore of hinges.
The two worlds
we know
we also know
the two worlds
do not rush onto ourselves
for we do not believe
cherished illusions

unable to form any image
have cheated us, already.

~

Citadels
enveloped in blurred sight,
Who walks there
sometimes—walking up and down
that someone has no legs
It has unhurdled existence
indestructible
invisible
it pulsates within us—no sounds, no echoes,
We wander haphazardly
since time unknown
to seam our ashen anxieties
but is it true our eyes have
blinded us?

~

In delirium?
In delirium creators create:
imprisoning the entire universe
in the grip of tiny partials
salvaging the armless poet
from the inexplicable deluse.
On a plain sheet of paper
spreads the entire universe
what you perceive as filled
I perceive as void and still

enduring decay that surrounds us, seizes us
Fear of fire tames us.

~

Far from ourselves
we explain away a sensation
in deep pain
our thoughts imagine a new occasion
not necessarily a discovery. Such pains
are black edges.
Nights crave for
our earnestness; worries on our visage
truthfully bear it out.
Seeing long enough
to unmercied end
yields illusory drowsiness,
We pass into them as they pass unto us.

~

Homogeneity
comes across multiple images
that overlie;
The successive moments of life
reality juxtaposed along illusions
our movement towards an end
the beginning tinged with a fusion
we remember the movement, not the end.
The reality stands afar
Illusions club us with counter-illusions
nothing stands nullified

The deeper psyche guides us into realms
of the unforeseen—
Digging goes on and on.

~

So often,
our ears and our eyes don't match
unfathomable states our mind carries
seek an exit outside—
Solemnity hangs in limbo
Diversity brings us hopes
in disarray.
Our reluctance
makes us unbelievers;
Under the latent surface
lurks a sense
chagrining us—
The indifference of the world
of our collective presence
makes our existence complete nonsense.

~

In man's defense
illusions have never been invented
ideologies act as secret enemies
justifying rationales for disorders
mussed and dishevelled in old clothing.
Life—a squeezed story, just now
all that is before us: our eyes,
have disappeared

Elements rejoin, claiming a
new revelation
We scatter it hurriedly
hopes linger no longer.

~

Beneath the roof that sags
we experiment,
Here is nothing in it,
really nothing.
Don't build castles in the air.
Good, old times are gone, for good
it's time to succumb
to do the needful—say adieu to.
In the meanwhile, will sail
a strangeness, elusiveness.
You ask for proof
there is no proof for heavenly bliss,
it comes from chance.
A virgin's greatest dilemma
beloveds too can have evils
evil-less shelters.

~

Mind and imagination:
a whirlwind of clash
don't keep with you
what is going on
Going back is a way
this is only to assure.

One visits the same
scene, inadvertently,
The scene keeps to itself—
the desire to ride illusions
in vain.
And the other—
not visiting anything the second time
yearns for everything to get back to it
is acquired; it is motiveless.

~

Arduous coherence
A struggle unto itself
spinning out at the end of
its meaning; keeping the
the exactness of meaning.
Noises cease to distract us
we go in for quietude,
Rolling us into our own
it is a stage of self-medication
filled with
an inspiring community of
incoherence, now hazed over
Light falls
darkness of the moment—
of no value.

~

Who walks
side by side
there—in the distance?

Nothing lives there.
Who has moved forward, so quickly?
Unfulfilling acts of glorious fabric
of moments that never last long
cannot vanish so fast;
These move and move and
then move again
looking at us, perfectly and precisely.

~

The fleeting and the infinite;
The perfect idler sways away
shrouded with melancholy
moving on a path
crowd has destroyed.
Symbolic values of this path
move as our illusions track
larger and abstracter things—
things without bound—
of the irretrievable past—
accumulation of uncertainties,
indecipherabilities, indecisions.
Let us be truthful to our experience
The paths that crawl
tell us; these paths privy to
so many illusory waves.

~

Herded into anonymous masses
of realities

illusions sap our sense of
uniqueness; we human beings are
unique—our being unique confuses us,
Our uniqueness is so loathsome
so labyrinthine
Images of realities intertwined
with those of illusions
Our memory stores both, lustily
displaying these
when these are least needed—
background unsketched
figure superimposed
agog to come out.

~

The end,
nameless, timeless end
humming, without vibration of its
silent lips,
The etiolated song of dead era,
It was the illusion that
becknoned us, that
in shredded patches of our spirits
unmorphed by collective memories
sent us to our continuing stupor—
We end up picking innumerable threads
frayed in the grind of illusory realities.

Unhinged
but recoiling with pity and scorn
that fleeting sense of illusion

explodes like lightning
Its image—
muti-coloured happenings
an involuntary flow of emotionless
deserts, unpoetic souls inhibit
buzzing poisonous truths
unable to suppress a sigh
that flies upwards;
involuntarily; devoid of eternal
horizons and insights.

~

In one magnificent rush
thoughts flow to me as if
time in, time out has vanished
and as if my walking thoughts
search for illustration,
There are perils
in skipping from consciousness
to realities to dreams
There are pains,
in remembering what is
unrememberable
These will find their way
anyway.
The separation between conscious
and the realities and the dreams
illusions bring together
Things separated long time back
kindle a hope.

Melancholy

Inconspicuous sense
of worthlessness,
enfolds.
Splendours of God's
blunders,
Joys and sorrows walk
asunder.
Dwelling beyond its stir,
melancholic dormancy
shelters its walls.

Conflicts

Drooping echoes,
in a whirlpool of
groovy hollowness;
Everything stills at glum
unstructuredly.
Zigzagging life
self-propelling,
retreats—
A flaming coil meditates.

Mind and Desires

Mind,
an epitome of
failed dreams;
Thriving on
realities—
locked in.
Impulses
hobnob with
desires;
musing on
dishevelled dreams.

Contemplation at 11.30 P.M.

My eyes half-closed
Bouts of contemplation;
Anxious moments pass off
Empty castles of the room come
too close
and then drift far off,
Fringed hands inside
ripple.

The day closes
its chapter
Despondency grips me,
guiding me to its deepest repository
Insane questions raise their heads—
Can you live without us?

I sense the blizzard in
my restless mind
Blithe of
my existence's persona
spun into its solitary whirlwind.

I have mist
hard to resist
Voices among tears
contemplating shadowed fears

palely the woes dwell
the clock strikes twelve.

Mortal strife
moves past the day's happenings
Puny-headed people…
they fish in muddled waters
and still we adore their being in tatters.

Is My Beloved Dead?

Life confronts me with my dead
beloved;
Happy joys
she evoked each time I met her
Now all—a part of my heart's abyss.

Once
She was the river and
she was the shore
she flew; she halted
she stayed awake in me
Her purity melted into mine.

I know still
She reads my poems
she tells me I have not changed
she tells me don't change, for
she loves my poems' multiple meanings
she finds them 'wonderfully significant'.

Death has not ended a life
Finishing a tiring journey is no death
There is no death in her death
A blank sheet of paper
never guarantees
it will ever remain blank.

The ink dissolves
drowns in the empyreal associations;
Hidden beneath shades of silence
I gaze,
Her reflection
expands as I grow older.

Soliloquy

There lies
no future, no memory
Past can be so ugly.

You want me to judge
Nothing exists or remains
Past disburdens itself
quietly.

Solitude
sweeps scattered remains
An unknown bird looks
deep into the abyss.

Spaces; unreal
things dead long back
loom larger, straying inside
straddling soliloquy.

Thoughts
melt and crumple up,
A long road stretches backwards
We are led to the gateway of amnesia.

Futility

Some hands
reach out to me
in meek expectation
My hands plead guilty.

Destiny
has its own bridges
It cannot cross; in rapture
hands keep seeking the missed.

These hands
compel my thinking
in the wetness of emptiness
our aspirations meet an outrageous futility.

Meeting Points

Morning
mists gaze into distance
into the sky.

fearing
an unknown infinity
gulping these soon.

believing
in impenetrability
of curled horizons.

merging
into darker arrival of
an unknown, uncertain future.

Unknowingness,
uncertainness,
unveiled meeting points.

Helplessness

Every night
dreams keep me alive
I fear my own shadows, which
might limp out of me, alive.

They still do come
carrying dead shapes of my desires
She once told me—
living loveless conquers desires.

Coolness of the night
discolours its darkness
A doleful melody that once was
confirms coming of another harshness.

Every torment
I welcome; mirror of future, graphic
Like you, I too succumb to it
I cherish my daytime yearnings.

Reflections

Night lingers a while
Silence of stars multiplies
Morning knocks at
Our conscience, accidentally.

Everywhere
only middleness seems visible;
no separation
no reunion.

Night, like
fatigued kings and queens
sees a life of something else
where swills none of its reflections.

Amnesia

Warm remains of forked night
Uncomfortable remains of
pre-dawn murk
Knots of unmemorable
Layers of dreams fail to open up.
An unremitting
aimless effort—guests come to us in
from deep slumber an
unremitting aimless effort takes
over us.
On waking up early
morning, tightly-knotted amnesia
rids itself of the mystic intrigue
that never was. Perhaps.
And yet,
the hollowness of incoherence ails
the amnesia—it's withering—
A pleasure or a turmoil,
cancelled in another guise.

Introspection

The hour has just struck
One should pause for a while
and ask—what introspection is all about?
There are new meanings
into what one sees or fails to see.
Drag those meanings out
and measure the falsehood of truths
or truth of falsehoods—beneath the meanings
just dragged:
Akin to walking a concrete jungle
where everything seems ensnarling
and never-ending like
the self with its riddling infinity,
infinity, more awe-inspiring
than anything else.
Something is hanging
for too long, there, in the middle of the air,
wriggling fugaciously;
In incontinent embraces of introspection,
its meanings search out for new doors to enter.

Inside the Castle

1

In the bewildering world
I will prefer to stay nameless
So many do so
Perhaps we all are helpless
before Him.

2

My grandfather
a worshiper of Lord Shiva
died so restlessly;
I believe in Nietzsche:
we don't need God
a dead God is not worth our worship.

3

We all surround him,
So eager for success, but
Have you ever bothered to know—
He hates your foul vapours
and not without reason.

4

Howling of grave winds
has just ceased
Go and rest; kill the howling
of dead winds inside you
lest you kill yourself.

5

It is a party
There will gather a group
chattering over the death of
the coming morning.

6

Don't berate others;
One day they will escort you
in your last journey,
Remember that—
be a good human being.

7

You, so close to him,
Don't poison his ears
Never forget—he is his own man
He hears you.
And then he thinks.

8

Beards
don't hide a foxy face
If obnoxious earlier, will be
more obnoxious now.

9

Sliminess
wouldn't take you far
Your wife—a game and
futureless children
will remind you of that always.

10

Don't think
you are too smart
That stray dog in the street
wagging his tail
knows your worth so well.

11

Light
be part of it
Darkness be part of it.

12

Love darkness
don't hate it
Never forget
you flew out of it.

13

This is a poem
not merely words and ink
An umbrella
gathering you
from womb to tomb.

14

Issueless teasers—let these
not strike you
Have you not made these
alien to yourself?

15

Over scotch
contemplating
the happenings of the year,
my wife in the kitchen
figuring not in my contemplation.

16

Alcohol
gives back to me
my ability to enjoy
the wild raving of my lunacy
my solitary ramblings.

17

Soliloquy
I flicker in fantastic shadows
The multi-layered fog removed
and I pen verisimilitudes
of my diabolic mind.

Merger

Evening suddenly dims,
Different versions of truth
walk past me, asymmetrically,
My dreamy aspirations drop
in decay—ruining my shadows.
From undulating, distant lands
overflow currents of floundering
life.
Elongated memories hail me
holding emptied burden
of weary stars ready to leap into
night—about to thicken—
a merger.

Mother's Womb

The blanket is the same
but we lie apart;
Having witnessed the citadel
of abandoning walls
we come out to meet
thin conspiratorial
hands; oozing out.
Trusted pile of light—
drips with hiccupping days
yet to shape up.
We wait to plunge into
the rivers we might not ford;
Still we fumble to and fro.

Can I Trust the Lines I Pen?

Why do I write?
To know myself
when I am deserted to myself
or when late in my life
having lost my memory,
I try to summon myself.
The lines I pen
would never deceive me,
So I trust, some times
you need a trusted ally
to tell you; you are not
as painted.
It will tell me someday,
when immutability of past…
passes through me, reminding me
fortune plays games I don't understand.
Hidden ecstasy
holds aloft:
My mother and my beloved
come together telling me
'We still exist—believe your lines.'
The lines I write
describe a land murdered long back
That was a land, I was born; I knew
diverse meanings of love and being loved,
That was a land, my shadows

shook hands with me,
that land is still alive.
A poor, devastated mother
who survived the pain of birthing
and the joy of nurturing
her son; possession and loss grieved
her equally; every land has dual meanings
I enjoy the duality.
In that narrow, dirty street
I waited for hours to see
those red, absorbing lips, those
mesmerizing eyes of that girl
who kept coming in my dreams
as silently as I used to wait for her
hoping she would raise her eyelids;
Silence of the lines has not opened its
lips as yet.
A moment comes
I refuse to believe myself,
Many moments come
I am tempted to open the doors
to decipher
if those unvisited rooms reveal
me to myself.
These lines
free me from my shadows.
I am freed from my past and
from my future ; from the dead things
I am afraid of, from the voices that
suffocate me, from the hopes that
allure me: the lines I pen enliven me.

We Walk Together

And the moon arises once again,
the sky has not blinded me completely,
stars awaiting a dream's open arms,
a slow song etching into my consciousness.
From that labyrinthine route of my past,
frays steadily a face—vulnerable and jaded,
I keep wondering who amongst us is lost
as flowered dreams melt away in icy realities.
Like a grim clamp of light, melancholy settles on
that face—history lays bare its cavernous blaze;
a thousand thoughts refuse to fall asleep
they hold nothing in their hands.
This room of mine is a whole world. I see
wrinkled secrets in the smallness of life; I turn the page;
a new story enters the pieces of past time,
shaping us from the pasts as we walk together.

History

Vague doors
feed on the intolerance
of the past;
Memories turn into dull
pages of history
struggling with their
un-ownness.
Through images that recede
let us reach out,
in all encompassing isolation,
to things that don't recede.
A face, beneath, reopens
justifying itself.

Awesome Being

Muddiness,
We abstract into an idea;
Un-lidded images
do break apart.

The unease of being,
on the edge of congruous
Meaninglessness,
lurks nearby.

Devoid of charms,
serene ugliness
sprawls,
Dwelling among friends
our hopeless movements:
raised fortresses
tell us; we are alive.

Seeking new lodgings
dusty clouds swirl around
in deep delirium,
We find the world maimed.

A cycle of cause and effect,
both manic with life
we wilt entirely, unsure
of our absolute nakedness.

A Cell

It is a shell,
a doorless, a windowless shell
you begin your journey in,
you will see the land
soon.
The wisdom of the ancients
all scattered,
all lying,
an opening,
a closing,
you touch without reaching.
With the zenith in your head,
you step lightly or heavily,
you can't be visible all the time;
Oddly enough, no stars
have stirred so far,
that is you.
A life, so still,
in this severely cold world,
you don't seem to be missing
anything,
yet dilemmas shadow your
existence;
All along you are lost in
the ageing arms of your own.
Your problem is the problem
of ease,

tragedy of absence,
not convinced of its weight
you measure its distance from
an undisclosed space.
Echoes you create
illusion of an eclipse you hear,
yielding yourself to everything,
you bang your empty head against
that cell: a doorless, a windowless cell,
and find renewal of your riddling
madness
limping behind you.

My Birth

An old papal tree,
behind that ancient home
a freezing sense of inutility
Nebulosity flickering amid
clasping stars—restlessly calm
strangled pain.

Immutable peak,
out of the intense dark
my birth whirls back
Past melts into future.

Floating in the air.
echo of upheaval's silence
fails to conjure up
a question,
unable to
answer itself again
once again.

I, pain's reflection,
in depthless vacuum.

Unhappiness

Terrible unhappiness,
the wonder of it
Death wish pushed on us
Unhappiness and life
two sides of one darkness
Darkness is no experiment.

~

The outside pressing
Malignance of light flies
numbed with waiting for long
appallingly we feel like
a dying coal receding slowly.

~

Newness of the room
always the same
vying for the most helpless
thoughts of unending roads
keep amusing us.

~

Life needs big hands
to tackle its vagaries
What alters these vagaries?

Credulous and waning stillness
Answers really matter little.

~

Happiness is no virgin
Let us not suspend assertions
of existence,
dawning on itself is not
waking to ourselves.

~

In the idea of distance
limping away is no anodyne
Unhappiness is a secret art
though evolved so much
we still stand so still.

~

It stands
it sways where it stands
All that is left before us
is horizon
Our screams don't reach there.

Evidence

God's creature,
you know the worth of life
what does it mean to you?
or do you think the world was not
made for you?
or you don't want to ride?
you find life duplicitous.
You knock your days down
one by one
over and over again,
hidden deep in denial, wet
connecting the dots—
picture uncompleted.
Suddenly you become the evidence
It is heavy
its sound has no name
perhaps it does not exist
you will never open yourself again.
Hold back
you are real
Life—a house of cards
Nothing matters nor ever will.

Words

Words
Unheard words
intrude as
unintended secrets.

Words—
lifelong obsession
we follow these
without ever grasping.

From every corner
we feel a distance
False words
black out brightest days.

We pretend
to be broken, at last
afraid of what would
ultimately crawl.

In a moment
we all begin to ponder
why to capture words
one would never hear.

Great strength
in silence that makes us,
Words would soon assume
their own colour.

A Welcome

Walls, my dearest friends,
defining boundaries of my life
giving meaningful hopes:
meaningful light towards the tunnel
of everyone's life.
Sometimes, I proceed towards the walls
like walls proceeding towards myself,
We meet somewhere, appreciating
each other as if
we never knew the game plan.
Let me now reach out to images
let me hug darkling images;
darkling walls, darkling myself.
Fingers move on soliloquizing,
you move on, I move on, they move on
everything moves on…virtually everyone—to
a land of undivided memories where
posterity awaits—a magnificent orchestration
welcomes us.

Nietzsche's Poet

1

Early morning hours,
radiant hours,
And in those radiant hours
strolls the crowd,
non-believers; no God for
they think without God
they move.
A wretched man, a naked man
a lantern in his hands,
wearing no clothes: fearing clothes
emerges—howling—
'I seek God, I seek God.'
The movers and the gossipers
strung by surprise,
unable to think of
anything else
murmur:
'From where has he come? Has
he lost his way? Who is he afraid of?
Is he a child gone on a wrong path?
Is he a schizoid? Does he need treatment?'
Impressive questions
haunt them, the wretched

man forays unto them
They, in circles;
in vicious circles
they confront each other
they fear their annihilation;
they believe in no God.
His piercing look:
their sluggishness visible to its core
revealing a story on luminous men,
luminous women
on the move, everywhere, fearing
arrival of a madman
like a poet, afraid of nothing but
his poems
His poems must yield to the desires
and to the demands of a madman
who wears no clothes.

2

Furies of complexities
we pass through
An empty space
we drift through
God is decomposing.
Silence of the madman
breaks again,
A dangerous legacy, voices that keep
leaping up, again and again,

amid a crowd that prefers silence, that
admires its members, their puniness—
a dangerous voice.
'All of us have killed God, you and I
all men and all women have killed God.
We all are murderers of murderers; we
all are the murderers of all murderers.'
Agitated voices precede deep silence
so believes that madman
for he maintains the silence of
a poet. But he is alive.
Bristling with
calmness outside in the crowd
the sea, that stormy sea is at rest;
waves; calmed down but inside
they fear the poet the madman
is carrying.
That lantern has light; crowd fears
light; it sheds light on the crowd;
Those staying in dark fear light;
Wise, successful men fear madman;
Poet has virtues
contemporary world fears and hates.

3

Madman knows that
lies in the lantern the grave problem;
Kill it—how?
Smash it. So he smashes the lantern

into tiny, unrecognizable pieces
Does the problem fade away?
No, it arrives at right
time; till it comes it wanders, in limbo,
The madman has come too early; an unripe
time for him to come. Consoles the poet;
'Does light not take time to reach earth?—do
thunder and lightning not absorb time to
strike?—my time has yet to come; I have
arrived too early, much before my time,
Let me leave with my honour intact.'
And thus he leaves,
Later, curious crowd finds him
declaring the places God is harboured
as the graveyard of the poet; the poet
has been buried there
because of us—we murderers of all
murderers.

www.ingramcontent.com/pod-product-compliance
Lightning Source LLC
Chambersburg PA
CBHW032050150426
43194CB00006B/472